LET'S PAINT

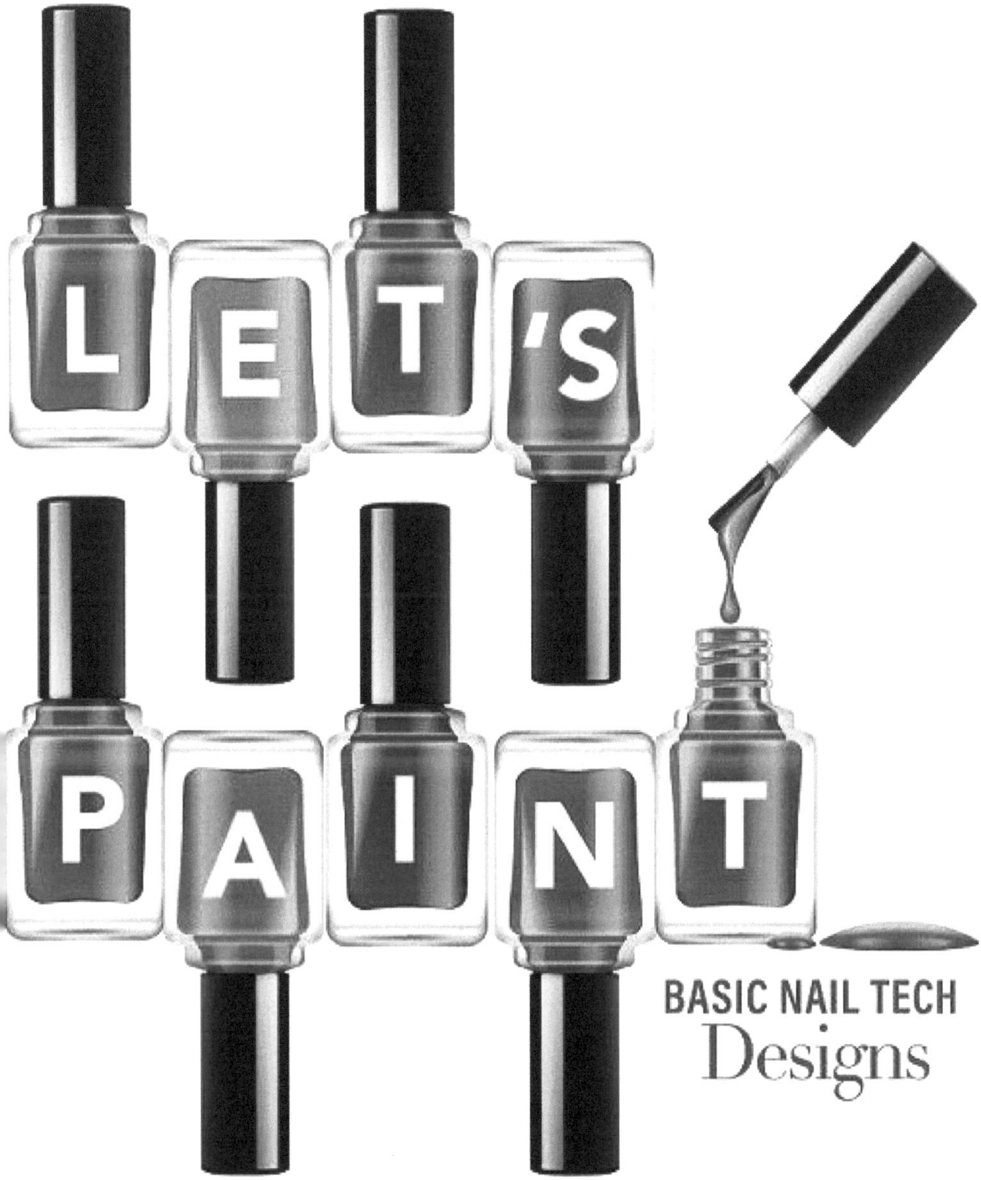

PAINT

BASIC NAIL TECH
Designs

SONIA MEEKS

Let's Paint. Basic Nail Tech Designs

Copyright © 2019 by Sonia V. Meeks

Email: gard3nlov3r@gmail.com

Printed in the United States of America

ISBN: 9781070801674

I dedicate this book to my husband, son, brother and parents who always celebrated my talents and encouraged me to always do more. I want to thank two of my best friends Tauheedah & Nichole for their support during this project. I also want to dedicate this book to my ten year old self who always believed more was possible and never allowed me to forget it, even as I grew older.

TABLE OF CONTENTS

INTRODUCTION

Let's Paint Basic Nail Tech Designs is an introductory to the basic beginning steps of nail designs. It was created for people who enjoy short nails and long nails. I've always loved getting a manicure, but as my budget grew and my finances decreased, I had to cut back on expenses. Therefore going to the nail spa was no longer an option. So I began to learn the basic techniques to creating an awesome manicure that made others believe I had just stepped out of a nail spa. Each lesson is built upon the next. I will teach you how to start with a basic nail design for different holidays or special events. After you practice each lesson, let your creativity explore and begin to create your own designs.

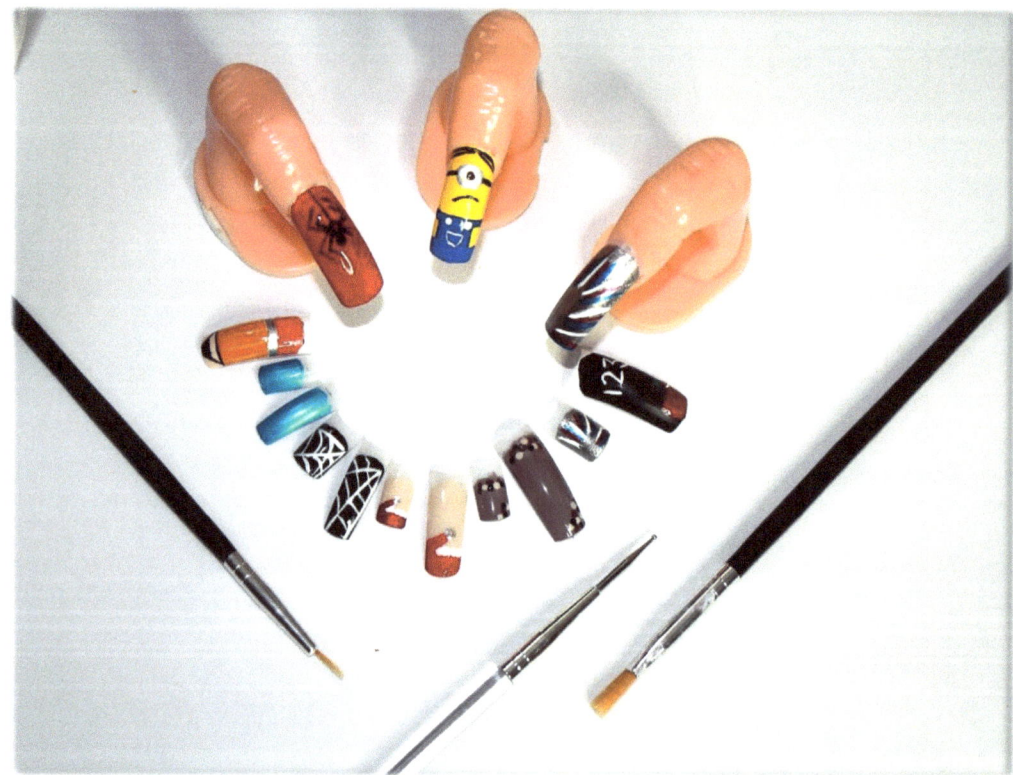

6

BASIC TOOLS FOR YOUR PERFECT MANICURE AND PAINTING NAILS

First step to a manicure is deciding on the perfect nail shape for you. Once you decide, follow the ne steps in order to achieve the perfect shape. Below are four basic shapes:

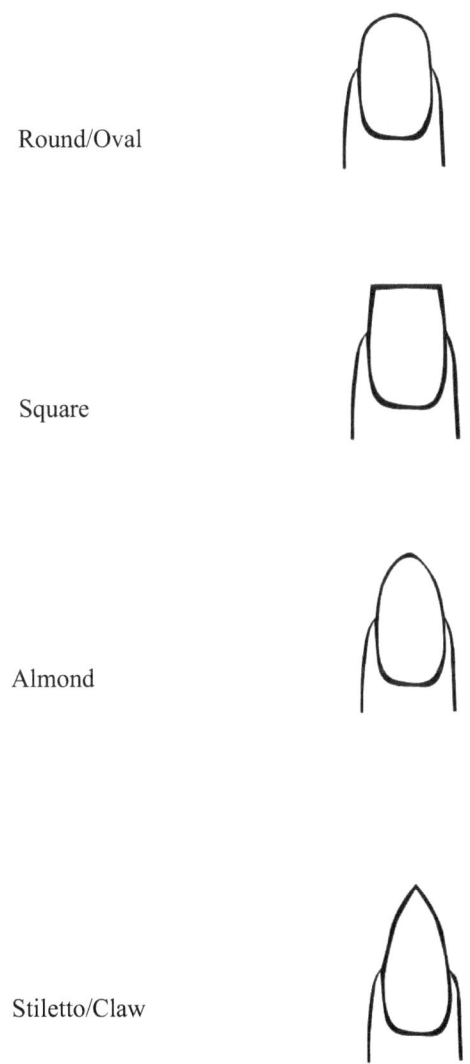

Round/Oval

Square

Almond

Stiletto/Claw

Items needed for manicure & grooming nails from left to right: nail clippers, orange stick, glass nail file and nail soak bowl. (Not pictured cuticle oil or you can use olive oil)

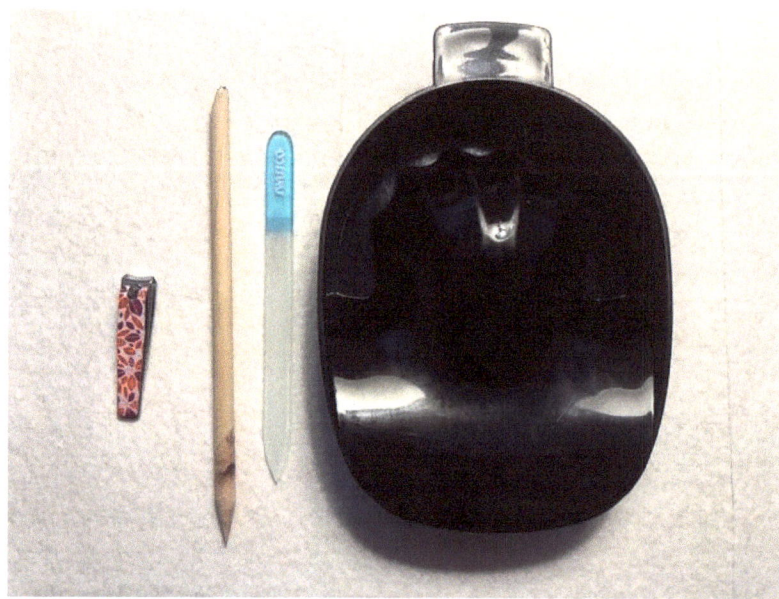

1. Fill your nail soak bowl with warm olive oil and soak your nails for 15-20 minutes. Wipe off extra oil with a paper towel. Fun Fact: Olive oil contains vitamin E which repairs damaged nails and promotes nail growth. It also helps to prevent chipping.
2. Next use your nail glass file to begin shaping your nails. Start from the side of your nail and file forward towards the tip of the nail. Repeat for the other side of your nail and the other nails. Fun Fact: Glass nail files help reduce jagged edges which causes splitting or chipping nails.
3. If you have any hang nails, use your nail clippers to remove them.
4. Now wash your hands with warm soapy water and dry with a paper towel.
5. Use the pointed end of your nail stick to gently clean under your nails. With the opposite end of your nail stick, gently push your nail cuticle back. Fun Fact: Pushing your nail cuticles back help your nails to look longer while also keeping them healthy.

Now you will learn the basic steps to start doing nail art. We will build upon each lesson until you are able to create your own designs. It is important to practice each lesson to be successful and comfortable with each technique. Each lesson will provide you with an illustration for people with short and long nails.

LESSON 1 -- Items needed for basic paint: Nail lacquer polish, acetone, flat nail paint brush, paper wels, and nail tee cotton swabs

Step 1: Place your brush at the base of your cuticle, flatten your brush and pull forward down the nter.

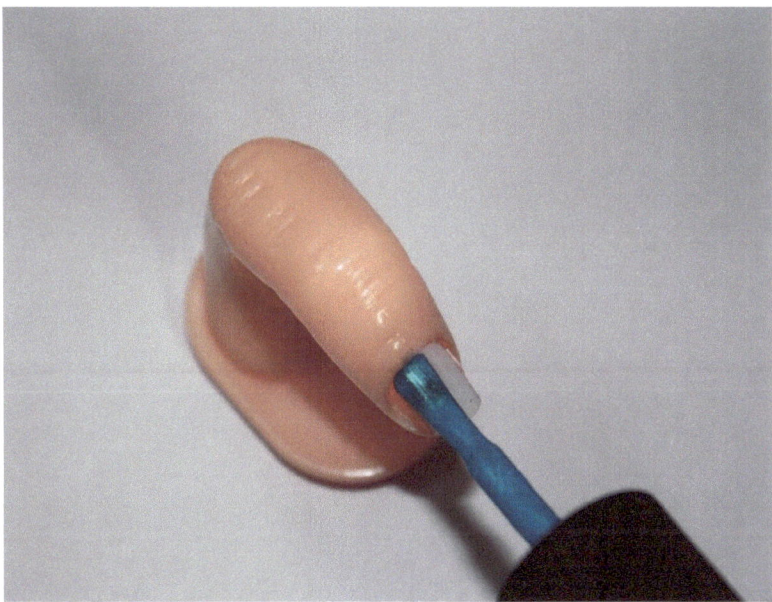

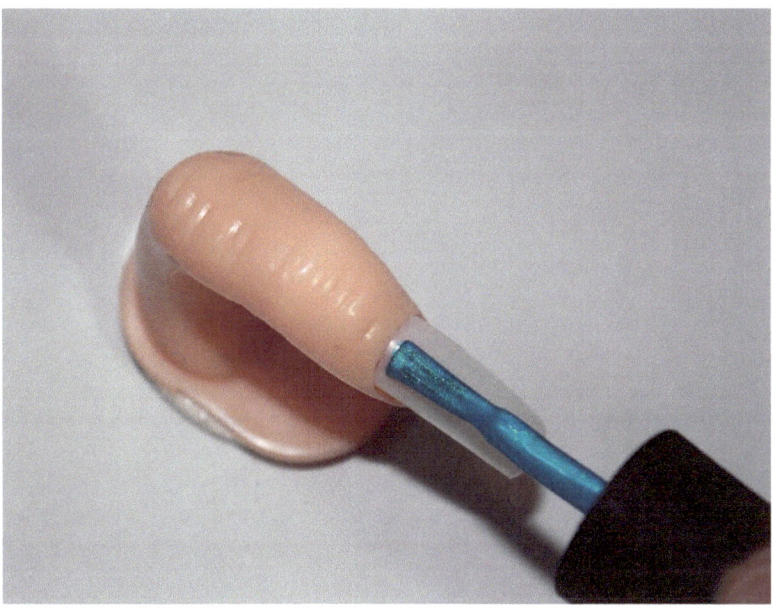

Step 2: Place your brush on the right side of your cuticle and pull forward to the tip of your nail. *Repeat step on the left side.

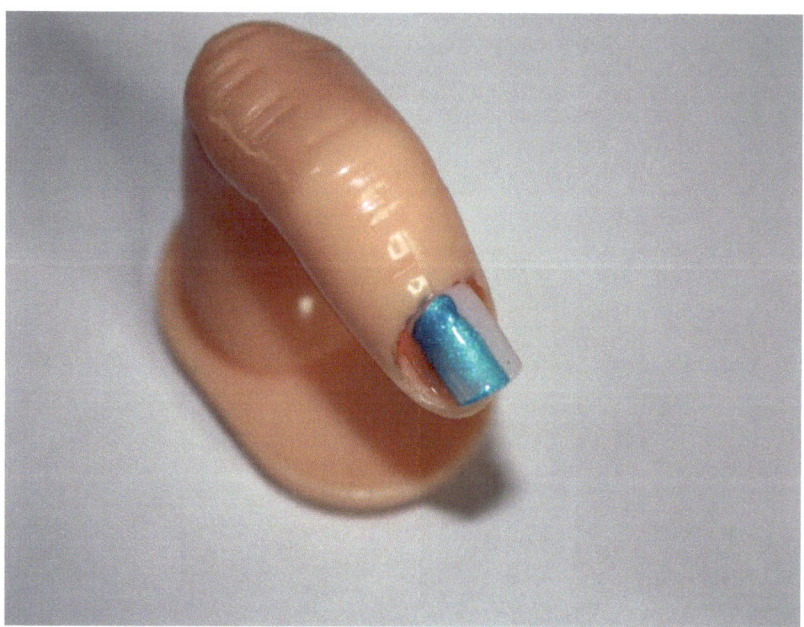

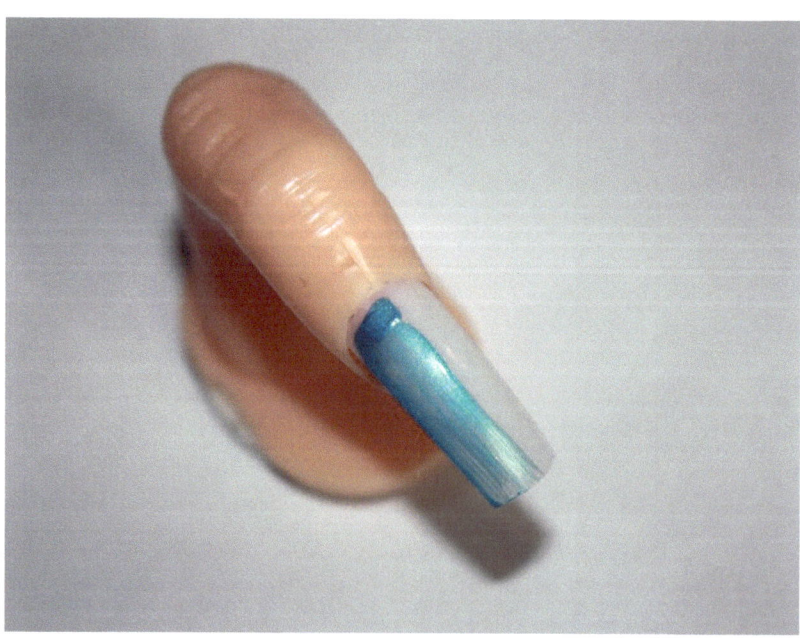

Step 3: Add an additional coat by repeating steps 1 & 2. With the flat part of the brush, seal the tip of ur nail manicure to look neater and prevents quick chipping of your nail. If necessary dip your nail tee tton swab in acetone and clean the edges of your fingers from excess nail polish

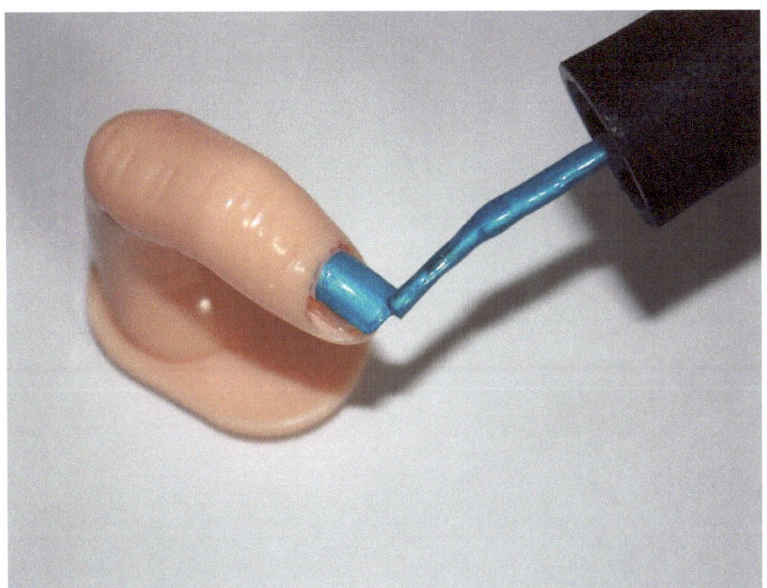

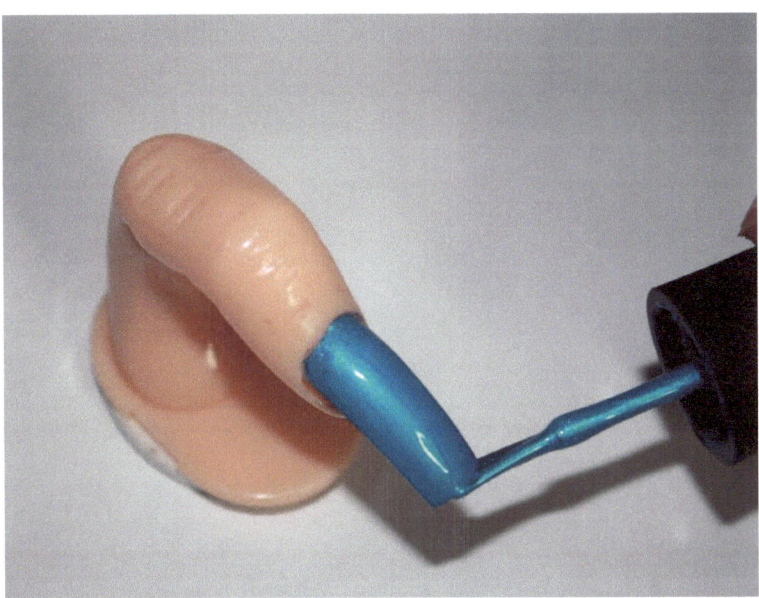

LESSON 2 -- Items needed for dotticure design: Nail lacquer polish, acetone, dotting tool, paper towels, and nail tee cotton swabs. *Dotting tools come in different sizes. For this design I use a 1.5mm

Step 1: Choose your base color and repeat the steps learned in lesson 1.

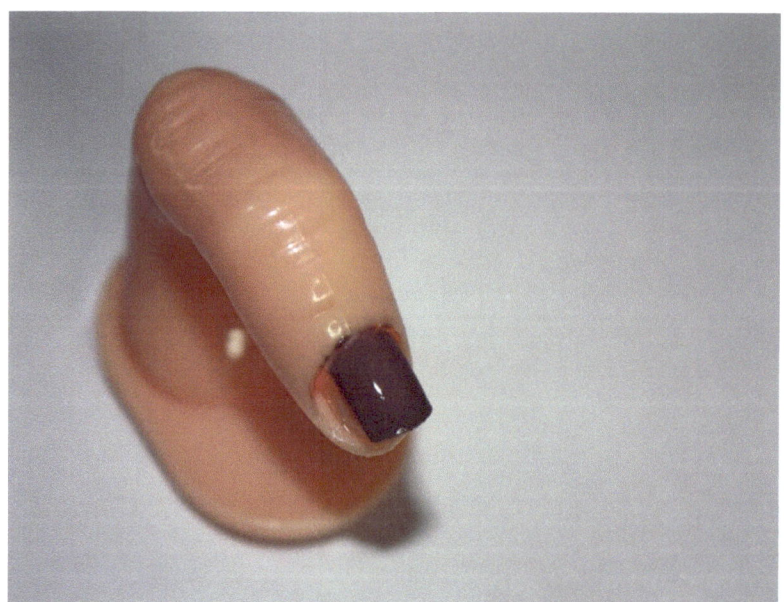

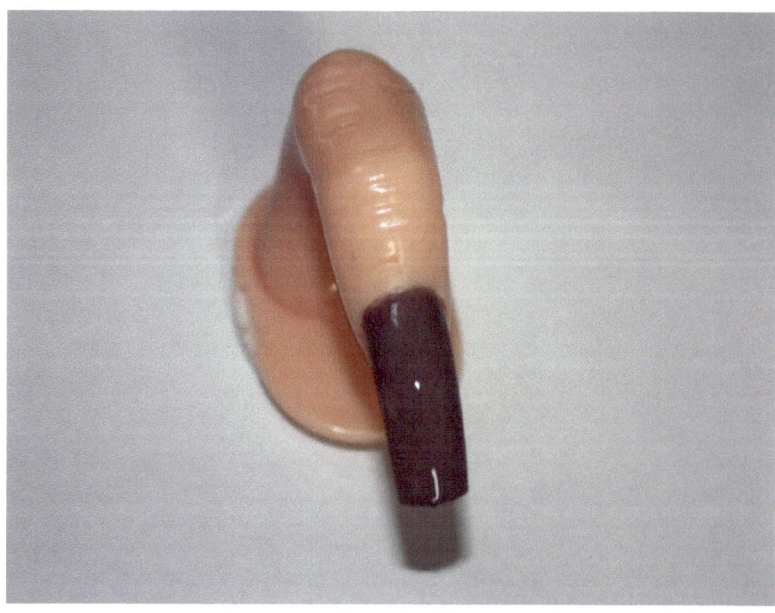

Step 2: Choose your accent color(s) for your dotticure. Drop a dab of polish on a scratch paper and ‚ the tip of your dotting tool in the paint. While holding your tool straight & steady apply to your nail.

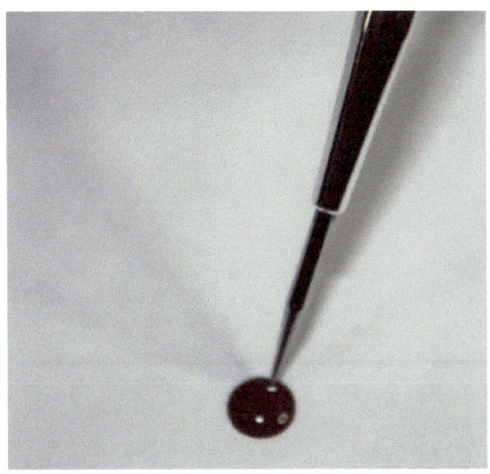

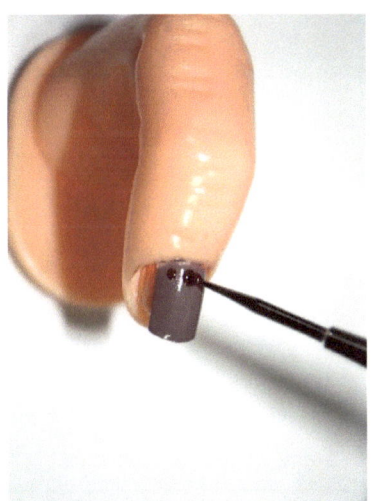
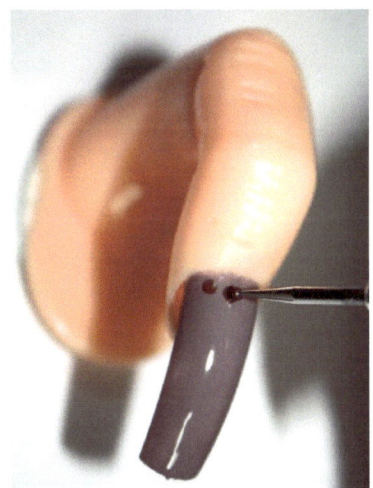

Step 3: Alternate your dotticure colors around your nail for the desired look.

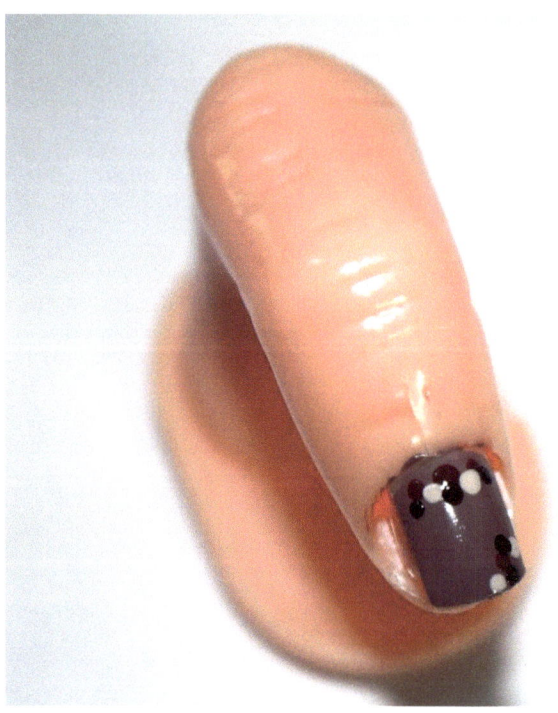

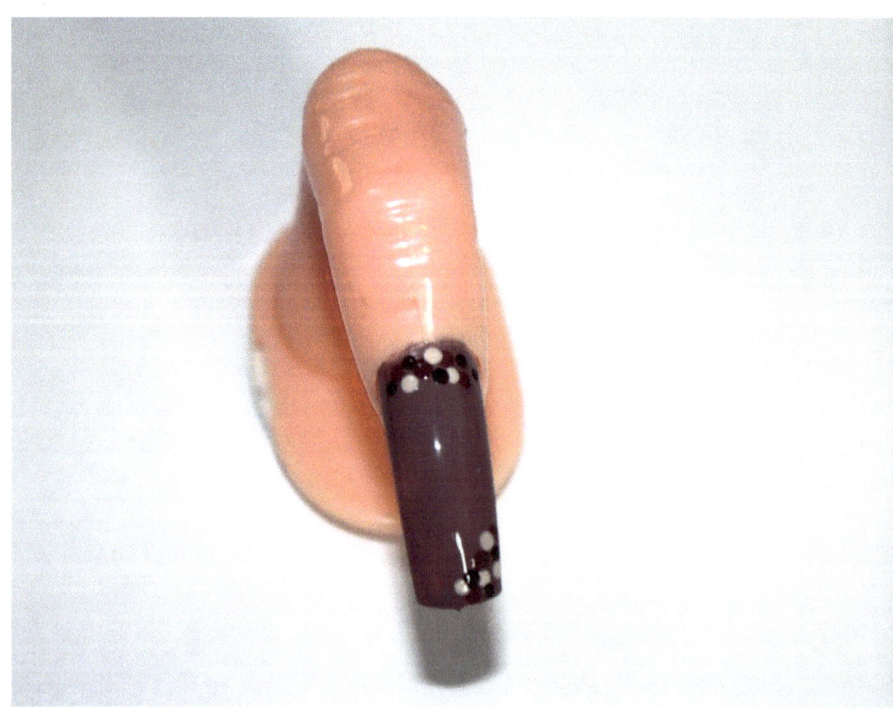

Step 4: Finish off your design with either a clear top coat or a glitter top coat to add some sparkle. Clean up the side of your finger from any excess polish using acetone and your nail tee cotton swab.

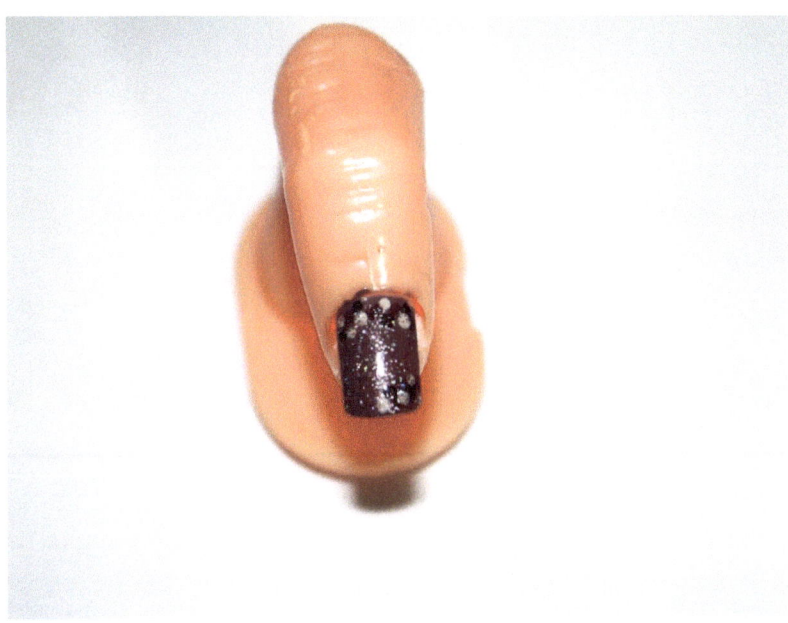

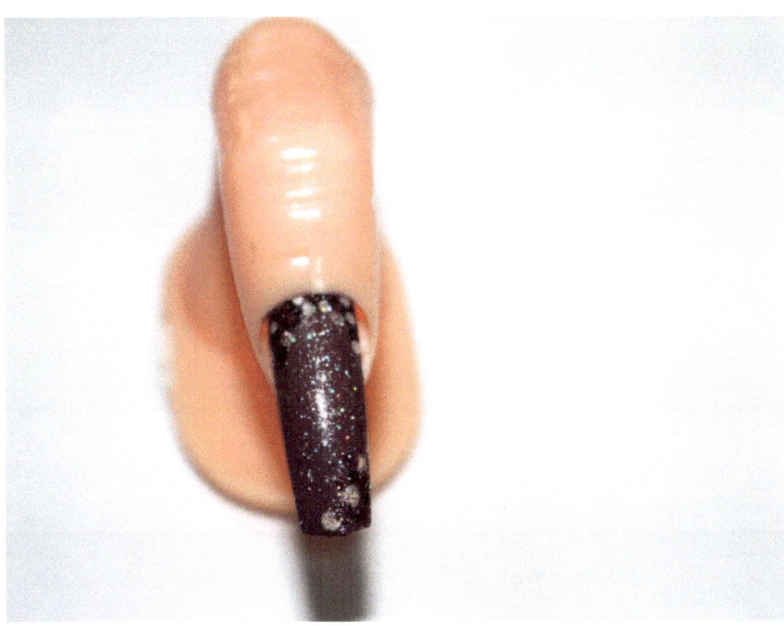

LESSON 3 -- Items needed for French manicure design: Clear & white nail lacquer polish, acetone paper towels, and nail tee cotton swabs.

Step 1: Choose your base color and repeat the steps learned in lesson 1. Usually for a French manicure you use clear nail polish or a light beige color.

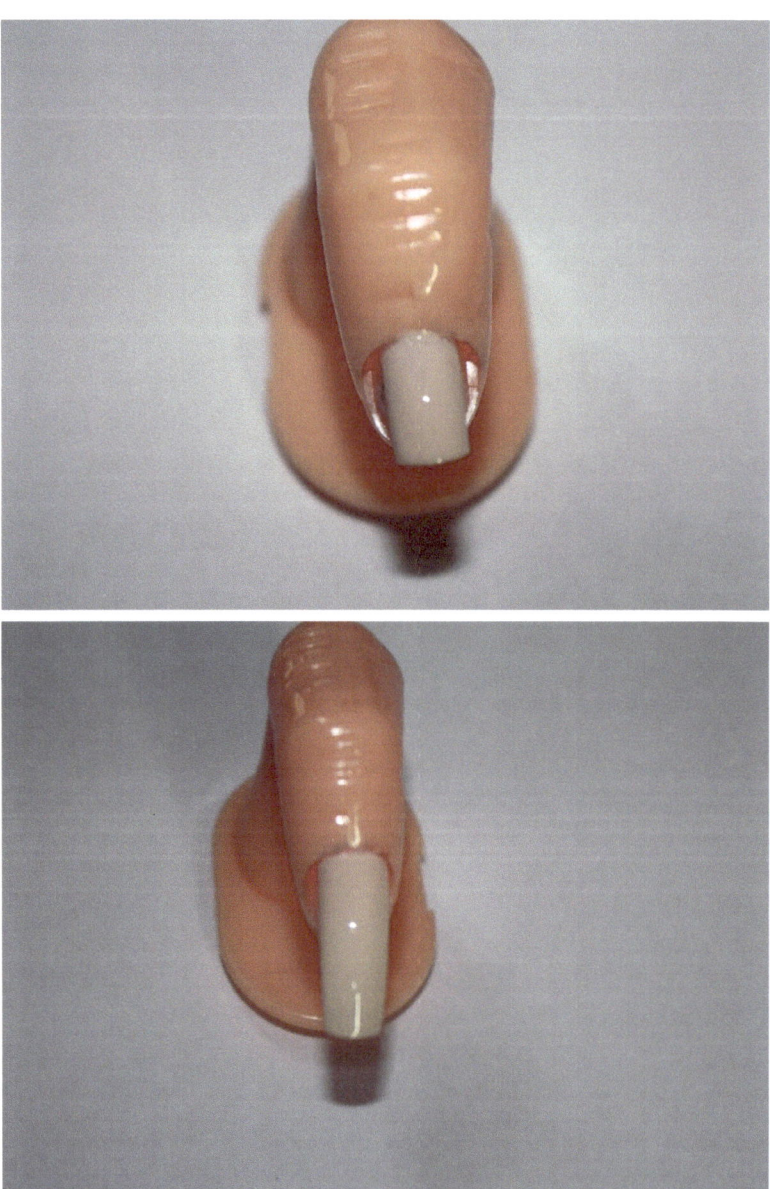

Step 2: With the flat end of your nail brush dip it in your white polish. Start from one side of your nail and lay your brush completely flat and pull your brush to the opposite side of your nail.*Repeat step to make line look cleaner. For the smaller nail you can use a small detail brush.

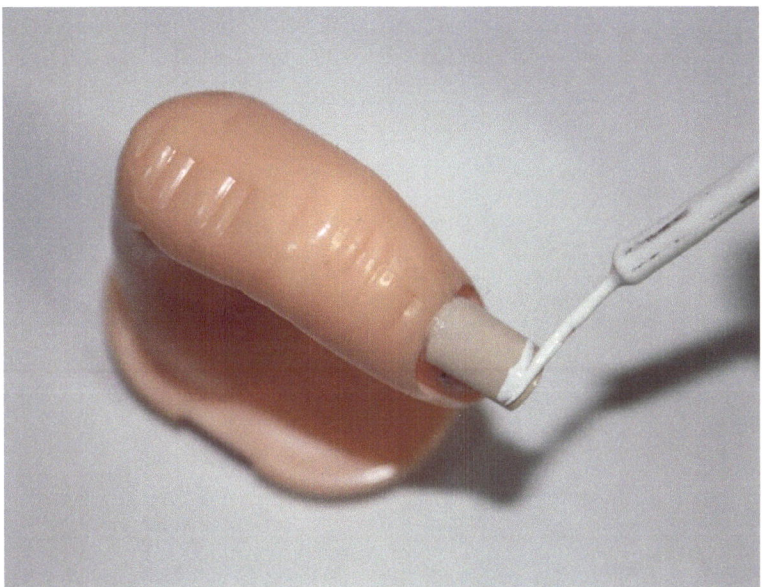

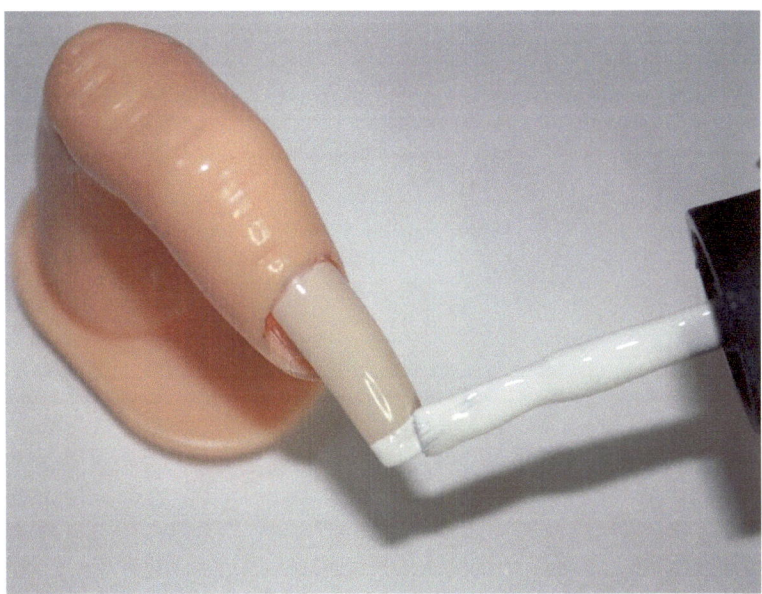

Step 3: Finish off your design with a clear top coat. Clean up the side of your finger from any excess polish using acetone and your nail tee cotton swab.

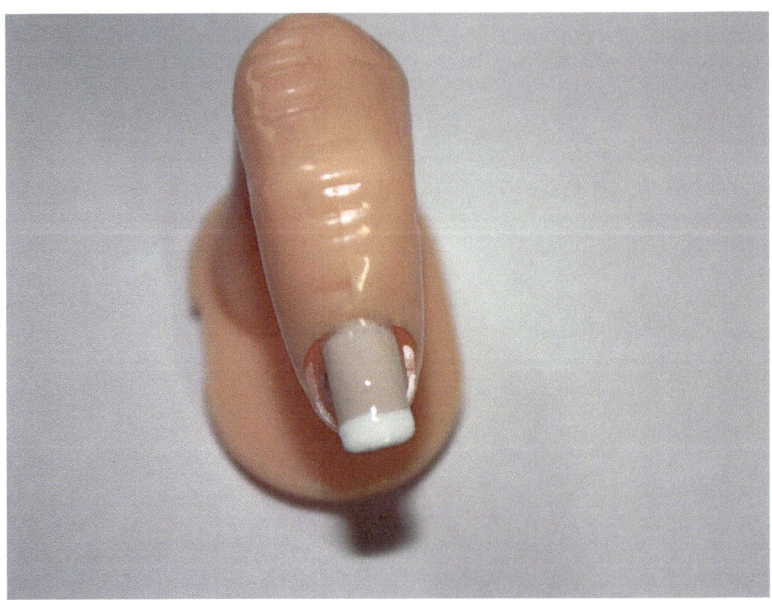

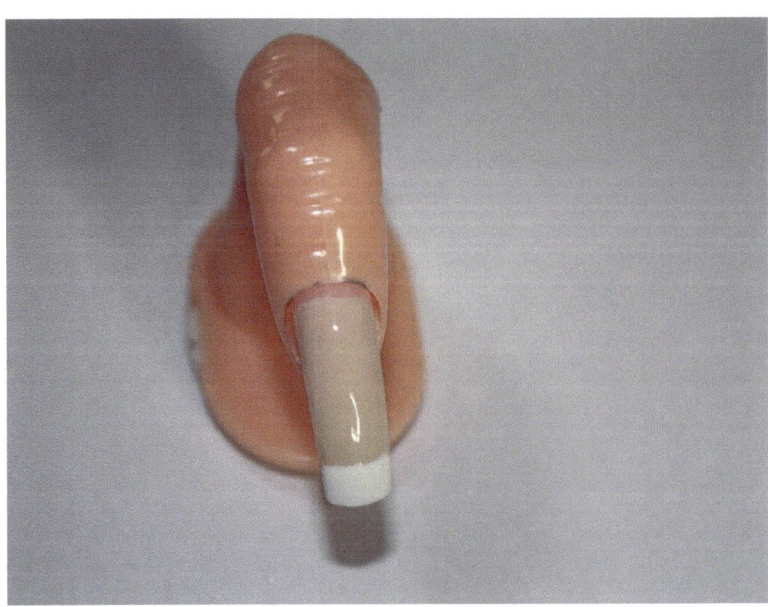

LESSON 4 -- Items needed for Christmas design: Nail lacquer polish, acetone, small detail nail ush, dotting tool, paper towels, and nail tee cotton swabs.

Step 1: Choose your base color and repeat the steps learned in lesson 1. Then repeat step 2 from sson 3.

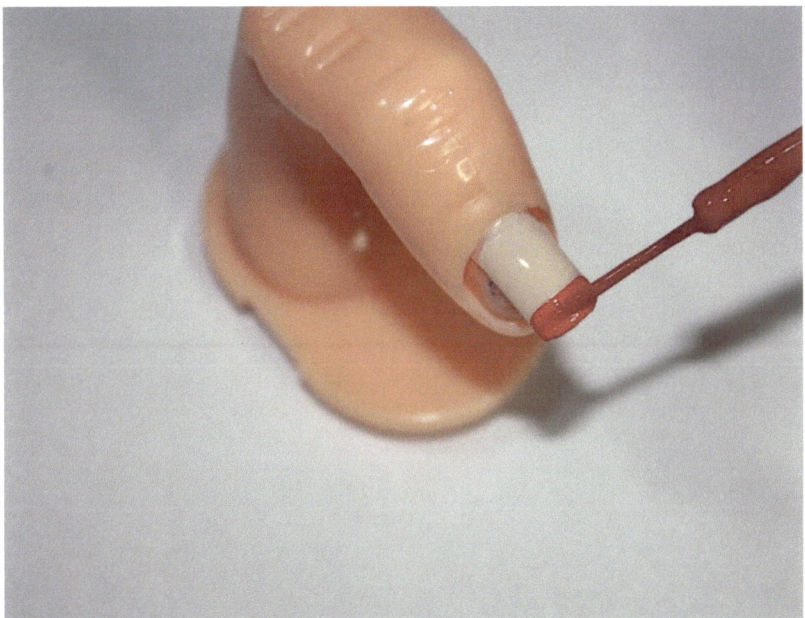

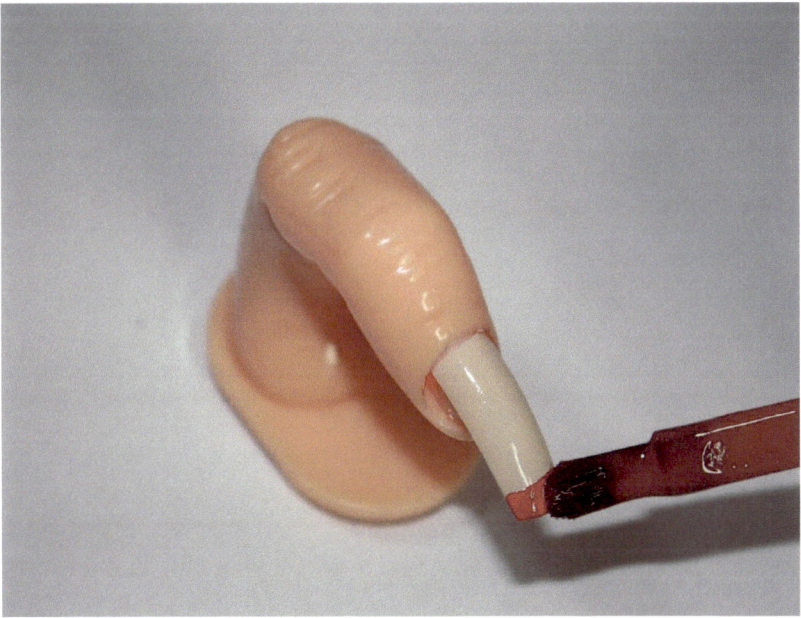

Step 2: With the same color you used for your nail tip, dip your detail brush and paint a line on the side of your nail.

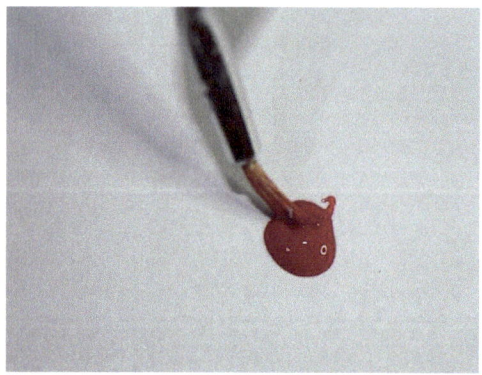

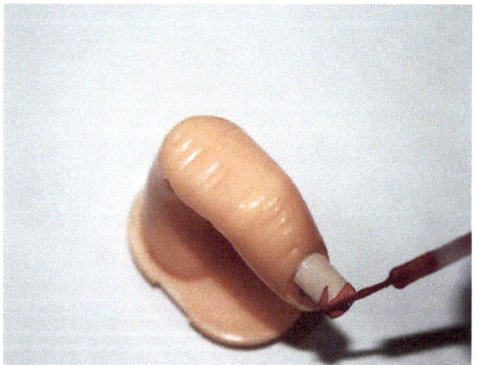

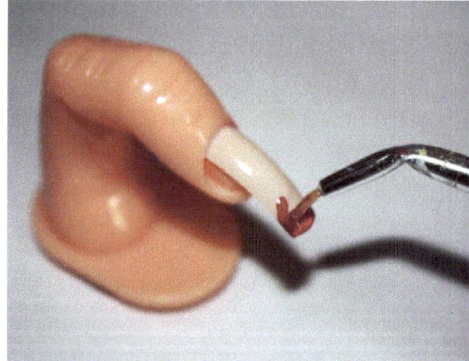

Step 3: With your dotticure tool place dots at the base of your nail tip. (As shown in picture 2 & 3)

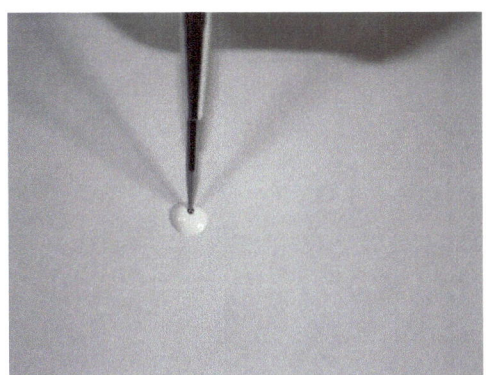

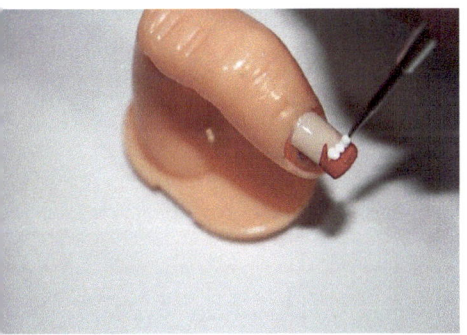

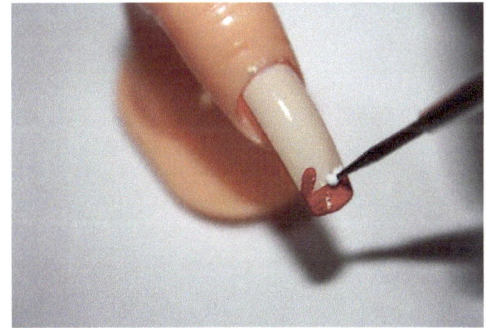

Step 4: Repeat step 3 with a separate color (silver polish) to complete your Christmas stocking ha

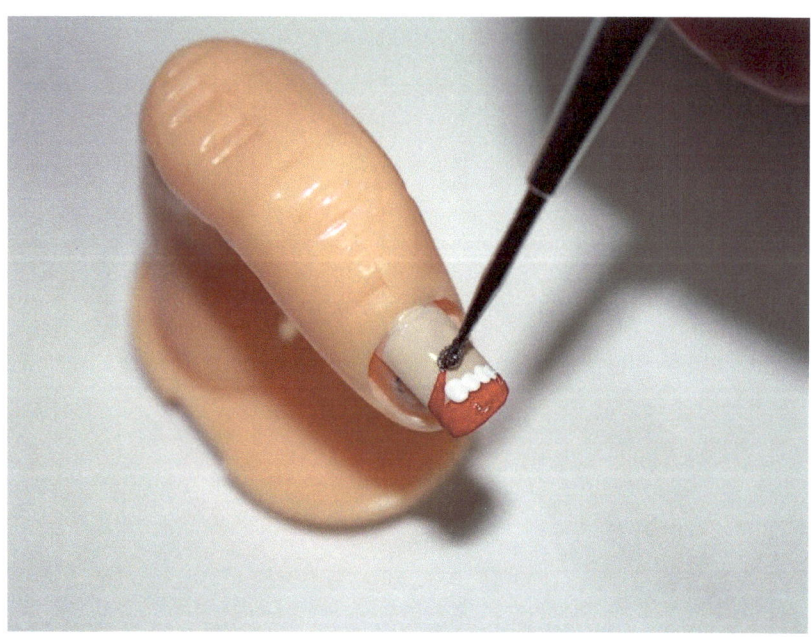

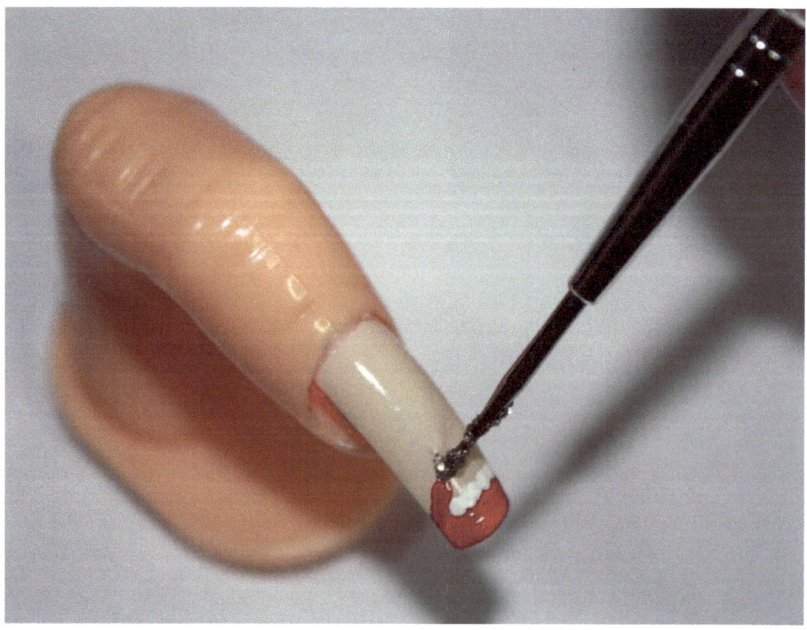

Step 5: Finish off your design with a clear top coat. Clean up the side of your finger from any excess polish using acetone and your nail tee cotton swab.

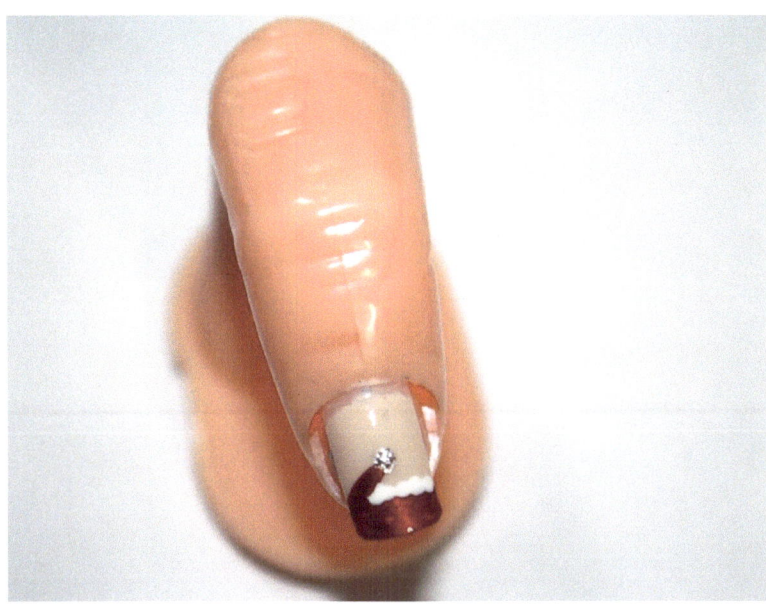

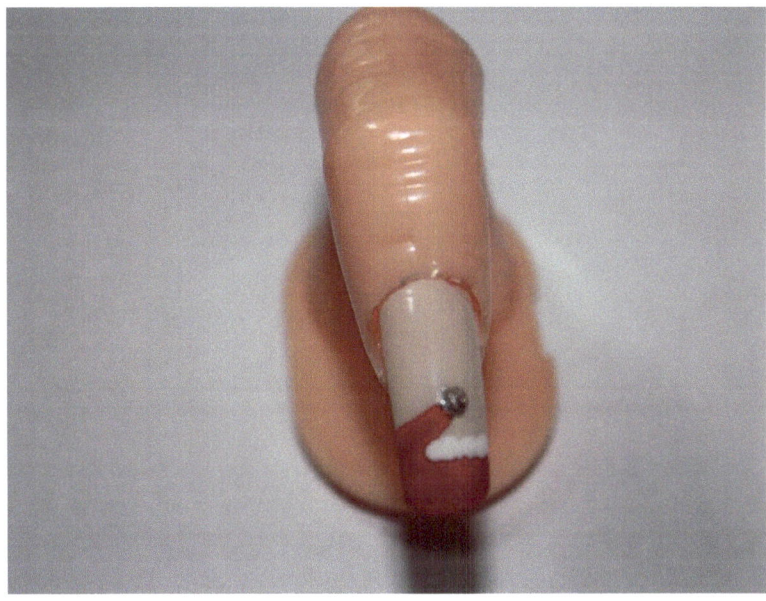

LESSON 5 -- Items needed for Fourth of July design: Nail lacquer polish, acetone, small detail nail brush, paper towels, and nail tee cotton swabs.

This lesson is designed for you to practice using a detail brush to create a firework nail design. Use the pictures as your guide as well as information you've gained from previous lessons. YOU GOT THIS!!

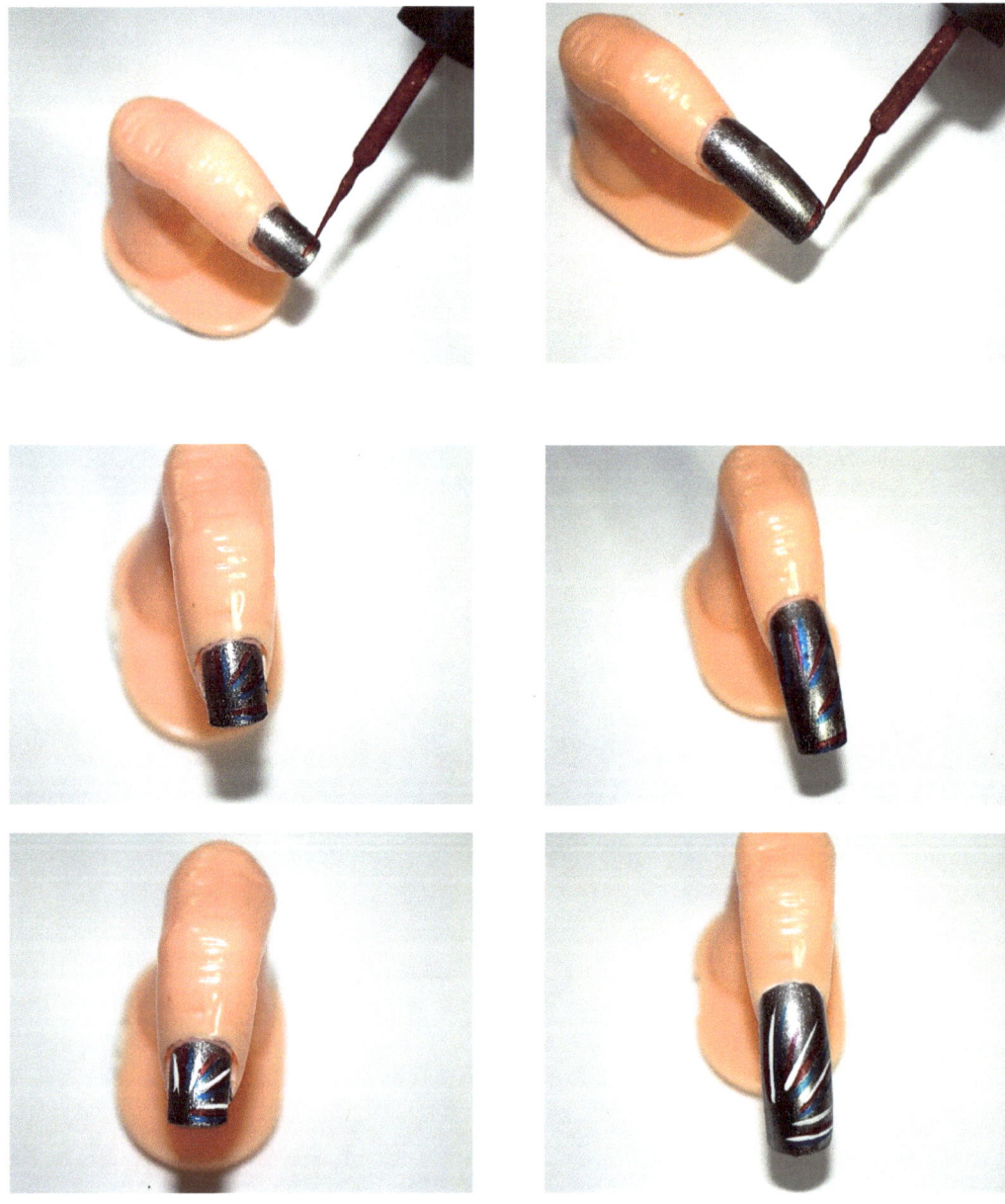

LESSON 6 -- Items needed for Halloween designs: Nail lacquer polish, acetone, small detail nail ush, dotting tool, paper towels, and nail tee cotton swabs. You've learned the basic techniques to ate this design.

Step 1: Choose your base color. You can use black as your base with a white web or white as your se with a black web.

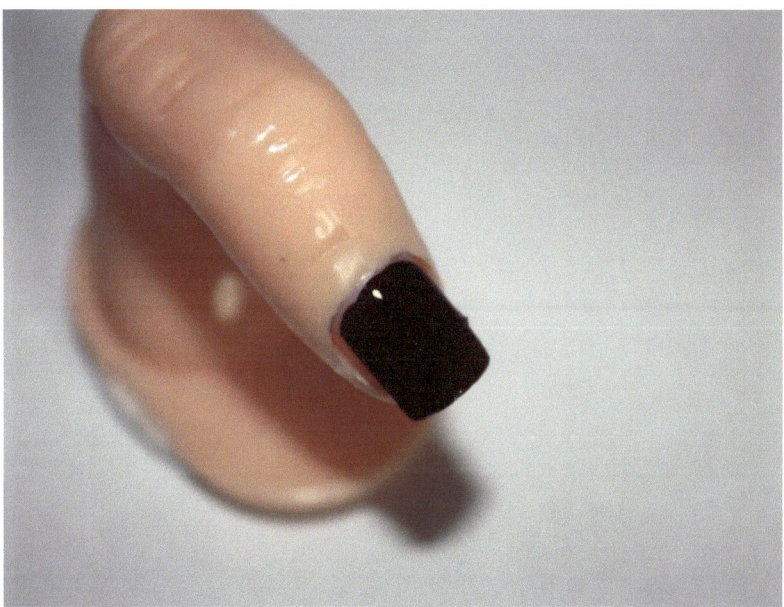

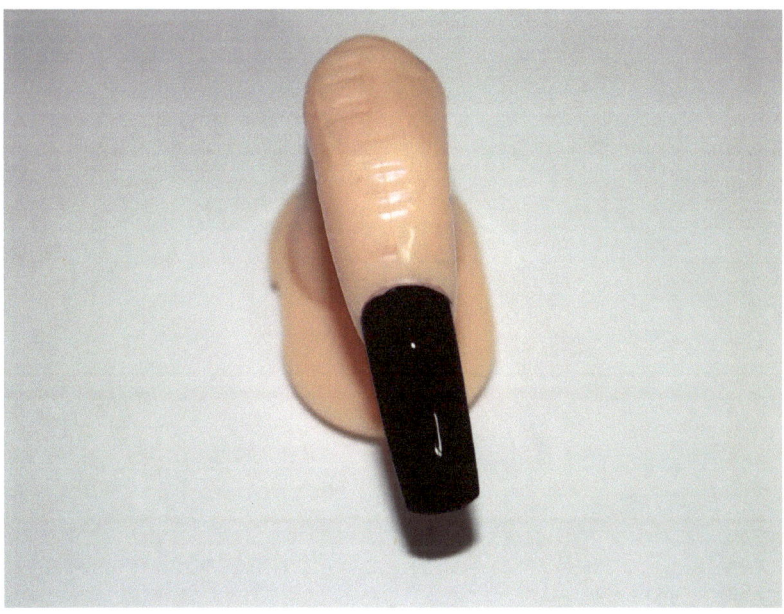

Step 2: Using a small detail brush. Start at the top right corner of the nail and draw a line to the bottom left corner.

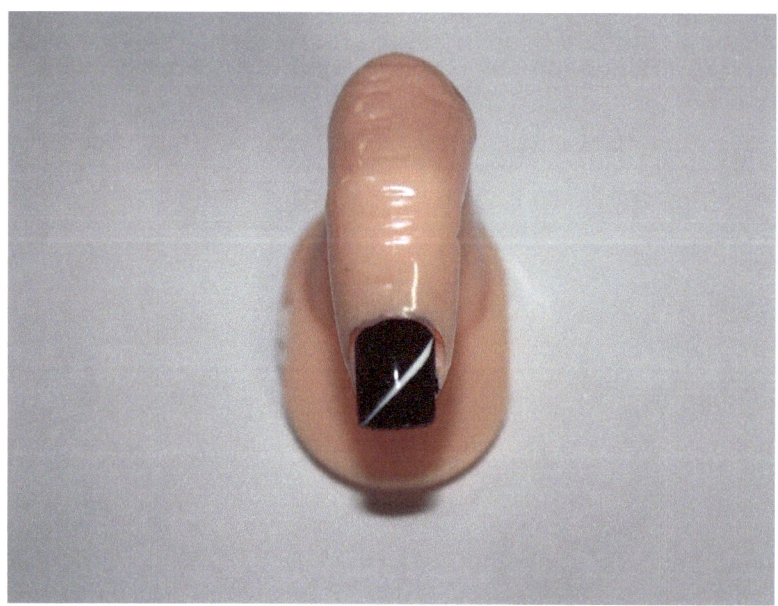

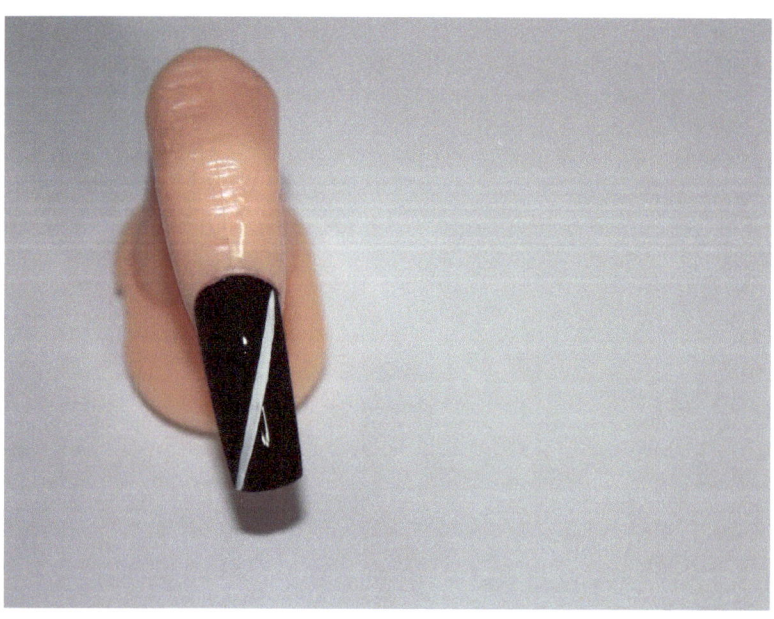

ep 3: Repeat the step you learned in step 2, but this time pull your line straight down and the other line the left side (NOT CORNER).

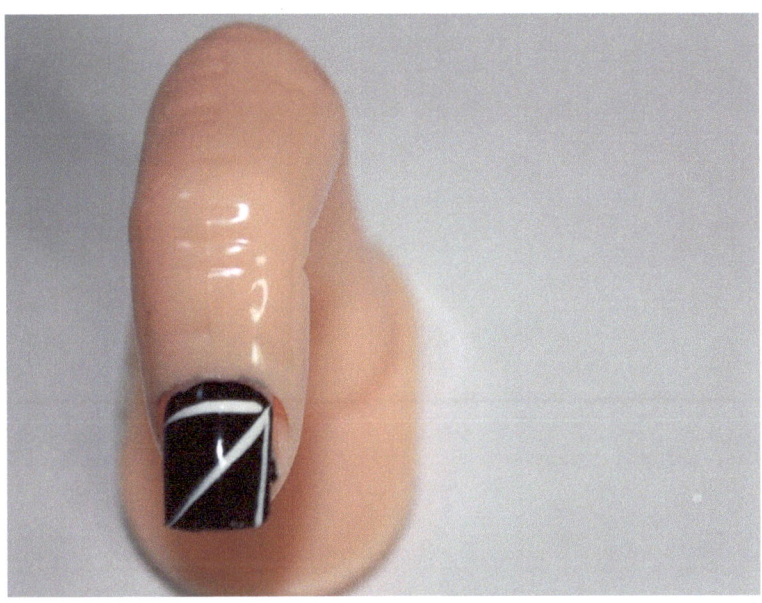

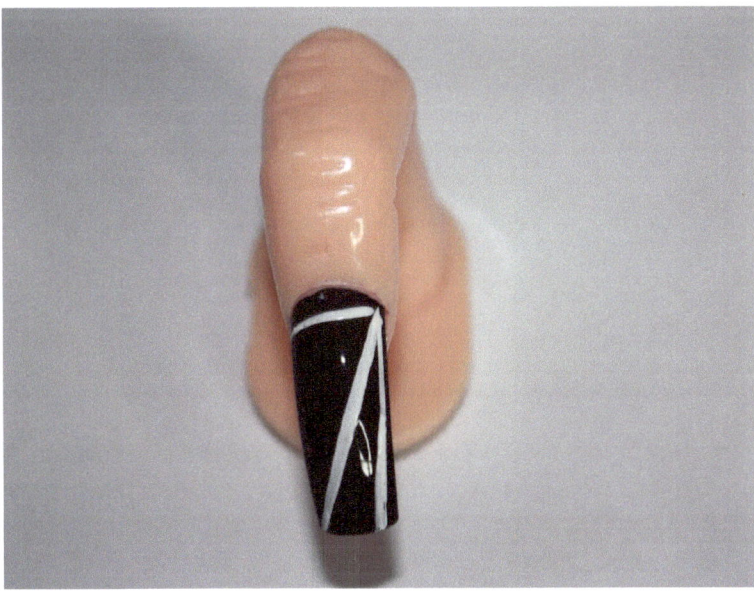

Step 4: To complete your web nail design, semi curve from one line to the next until you are at the tip of your nail. Finish with a clear top nail coat.

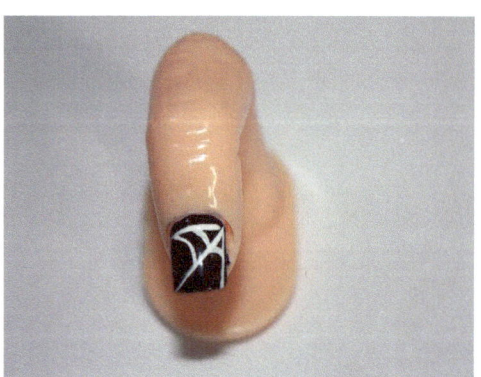

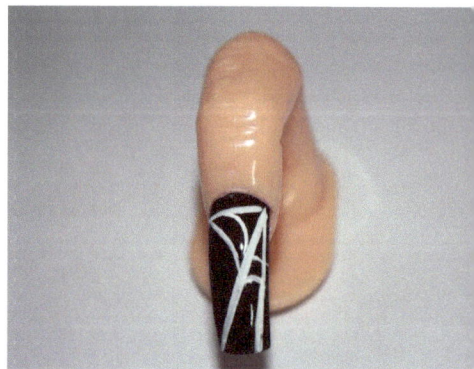

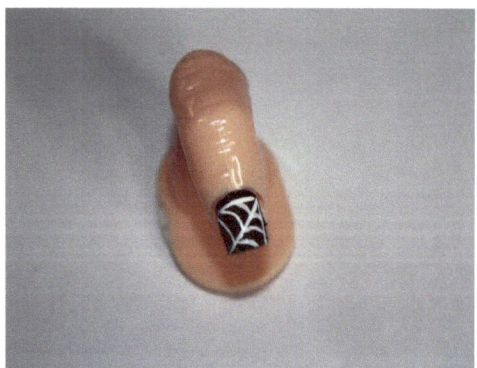

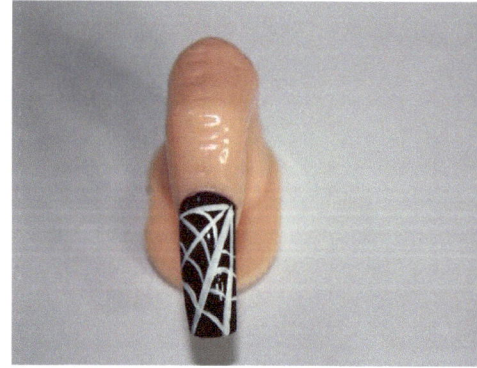

BONUS Step 5: If you want to add an extra pop to your design review lesson 2 on dotticure and practice creating the spider design below.

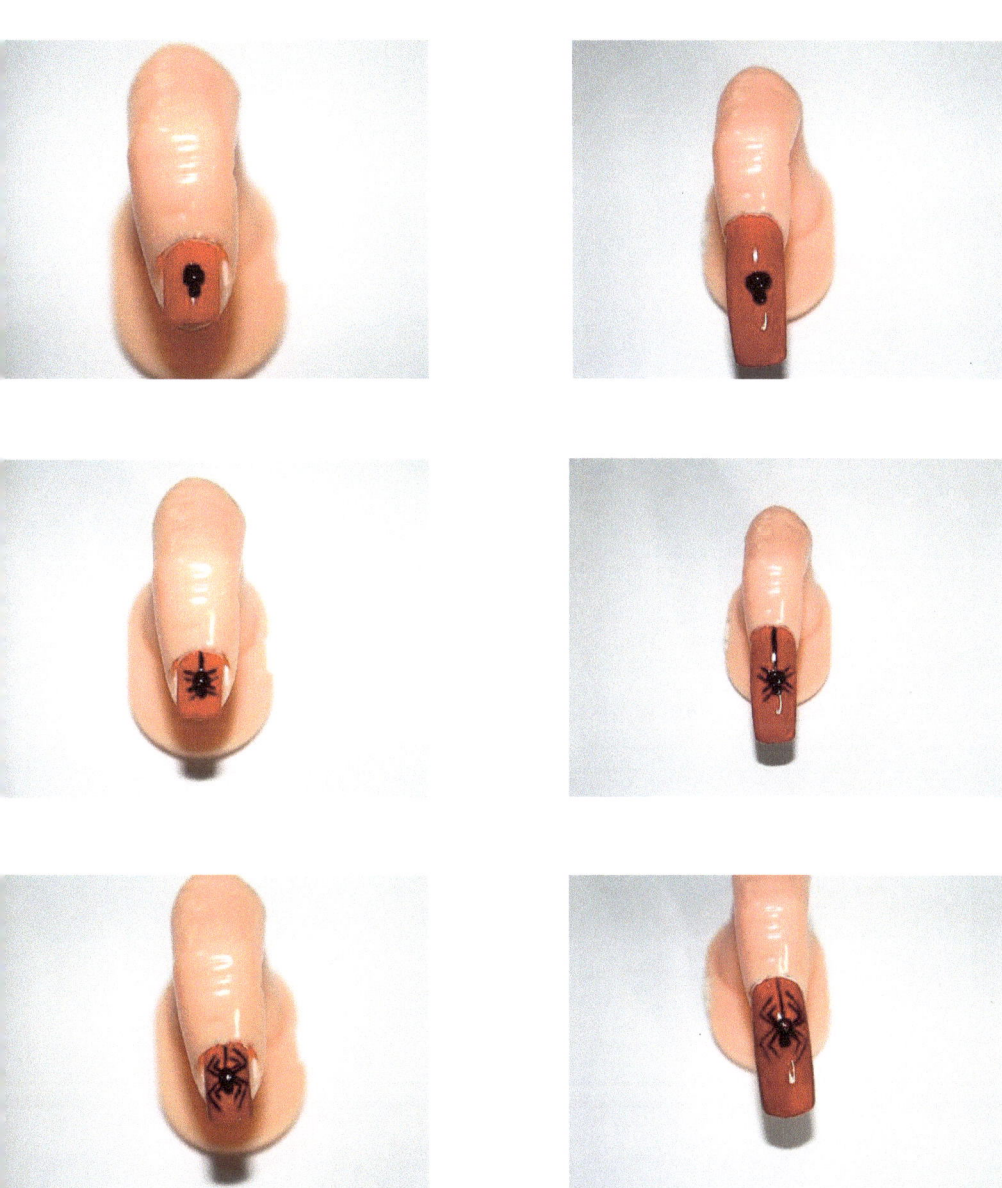

www.ingramcontent.com/pod-product-compliance
Lightning Source LLC
Chambersburg PA
CBHW040915180526
45159CB00010BA/3077